Urban Mission Field

A Plea For A Revival Of Missions

Urban Mission Field

An individual has not started living until he can rise above the narrow confines of his individualistic concerns to the broader concerns of all humanity.

Martin Luther King, Jr.

Urban Mission Field

A Plea For A Revival Of Missions

J.L. Shelton

Copyright © 2012 by J.L. Shelton
Published by Day 50 Publishing
Graphic Design & Page Layout by e2media
Edited by David Richards
Printed in the United States of America

ISBN-10: 0985228202 (pbk)
ISBN-13: 978-0-9852282-0-0 (pbk)
ISBN-13: 978-0-9852282-1-7 (ebook)

All rights reserved. No part of this publication may be reproduced, stored in a retrieval system, or transmitted in any form or by any means (ex: electronic, photocopy, recording) without the prior written permission of the publisher. The only exception is brief quotations in printed reviews.

Unless otherwise indicated, all scriptures are taken from the KJV & NKJV ™ Bible.

www.Day50Publishing.com

Urban Mission Field

CONTENTS

Intro	Introduction	Pg.6
Ch 1	The Urban Mission Field	Pg.10
Ch 2	Pre-Training	Pg.18
Ch 3	The Roman Road	Pg.23
Ch 4	What Next	Pg.28
Ch 5	Becoming All Things	Pg.33
Ch 6	Witnessing	Pg.39
Ch 7	Expectation	Pg.44
Ch 8	God's Workers	Pg.49
Ch 9	The Blueprint	Pg.55
Ch 10	Fisher Of Men	Pg.61
Ch 11	What Time Is It	Pg.66
Ch 12	Beautiful Are The Feet	Pg.72
Ch 13	Make Them Sit Down	Pg.76
Ch 14	At All Cost	Pg.82
Ch 15	Enlarge My Territory	Pg.87
Ch 16	Warning	Pg.92
Ch 17	Where Do We Begin	Pg.98

Urban Mission Field

Introduction

Introduction

When one hears the term *mission field* the first thing that comes to mind is a remote Third World country on the opposite side of the planet. While traditionally this perception has been the norm, a new day has come upon us. A day in which a land which was once so prolific in the sending out of missionaries has now become a land in dire need of the missionary. A day in which the journey of traveling to the mission field is no longer a journey, but a walk. A day in which the mission field has become manifest amongst us. A day in which the unsaved population among us has now tilted the measuring beams of righteousness, and the evidence of it is right before us.

Adultery, Fornication, Divorce, Murder, Abortion; these are just some of the iniquities that have become commonplace in a culture that is embraced by so many among us, and if we tell the truth, there is nobody to blame except for us… The Church… It's not that we promote or encourage such heinous acts of immorality, but it's that we tolerate it through the constant motion of silence. The fact is that we as the *eclisa*, the *called out ones*, have been given dominion. So the responsibility of moral discipline does not rest upon the government, or upon the ethics of a secular society, but it rests upon the shoulders of the Church, the very Body of Christ.

It is our responsibility therefore, to go into the world and make disciples. This was the GREAT COMMISSION given to us by our LORD JESUS CHRIST. We cannot wait for the world to come into the Church and expect them to conform, but we must *Go* into the world and make disciples.

If you pay attention to the command, it's a simple two-part process. First, the going into the world, which is the transformational evangelism that takes place when we *Go* into the mission fields and preach the Gospel. Secondly, the making of disciples, which is the ministry that takes place once they have come into the Church, meaning the fellowship of believers, not necessarily the physical building. Disciples are made through the edification that comes through the teaching of the Word of God and the administration of the gifts in which God has instilled within each and every one of us.

The *Urban Mission Field* is a place where some of the most beautiful outpouring of ministry can take place. It is a place where God desires to do a great work. It is a place that is crying out for the Gospel of Jesus Christ. *We must Repent.*

Urban Mission Field

Urban Mission Field

Chapter One

1 Corinthians 15:20
And so I have made it my aim to preach the gospel, not where Christ was named, lest I should build on another man's foundation.

The Urban Mission Field

The *Urban Mission Field* is one of the most misunderstood and neglected areas of potential ministry in our land. While many of our Churches are located right in the middle of these prospective ministry zones, unfortunately not many of them truly do anything to reach these people groups with the message of the Gospel of Jesus Christ.

The *Urban Mission Field* is usually the place that most people try to avoid. Many Churches decide not to plant in these areas or, they seek to re-locate away from these areas due to the obvious fact that the people groups that live within these communities do not have the financial stability nor the means to support what 21st century

Urban Mission Field

Ministry has become. This is an unfortunate and unspoken truth that exists silently within our Churches.

The reality is that we have been called to the lost and the biggest indicator that the Church has neglected her spiritual obligation is the obvious morally deprived condition that our communities are in. One thing that is for sure is that when the Gospel is preached, sinners are converted. We have been called to convert those who live like gentiles into what is called a Christian or a follower of Christ. Instead, most of the people who fill our pews and walk our isles every Sunday are people who have grown up in our Church or people who have held memberships at previous Churches.

Let's be honest, we have not been intentionally going after the lost. One quick scan through the people who sit on our pews and it becomes blatantly obvious that we have not been aiming at converting the lost but rather at conforming the church *transfer* member to our way of having Church, with the goal of increasing what some of our pastors have now started to call our "giving units" (membership base).

In short, our campaigns are geared at attracting Church folk. We post signs in our communities that say *"Come and Worship With Us"*. Now if you were lost and had never heard the Gospel, how could the phrase *"Come and Worship With Us"* compel you to visit a WORSHIP SERVICE at a CHURCH to worship a GOD that you do not know?

Before we can arrive at the doorsteps of change, we must first identify the error of our ways. It is not an opinion but it is a fact that we have failed our communities. The blame for this failure falls on no one except for us; not the Government, not the School System, but the Church. It is our fault. God has called us to bring radical transformation to our communities and He has given us the authority to succeed, but we have failed. We will not see the mighty moves of God that we desire to see until we address the issue of the lack of the preached Gospel in the *Urban Mission Field*.

It is not enough to preach Sunday in and Sunday out from the pulpit and expect change, but we must be intentional about seeking those who do not make it their intent to seek God. We must ask God to give us the compassion and the zeal to reach the lost. Sunday morning is not going to restore our communities. Church service is not going reach the young man who is on the block pushing crack who believes that he is justified because his *Hood Theology* that he has developed over the years tells him that God knows his heart.

There is a silent cry in our communities that can only be comforted by those who carry the mantle of the anointing. This cry can clearly be heard through the disturbing statistics that we read about. Substance abuse, violent crime, and the single-parent household ratio are just a few of the many contributing factors that give voice to this silent cry. These statistics cry out for the Gospel of Jesus Christ. The statistics are the evidence that people are hurting and in need of the message that God has entrusted within those who serve at His altar. If you want to know where to preach the Gospel, just look at the statistics.

We by no means resemble the Church that we read about in the Book of Acts. We have lost the discipline that Jesus passed down to those who walked with Him. Jesus was intentional about teaching His disciples how to reach those in the mission field. He sent them out to proclaim the good news and bring healing and deliverance to those in need. He set the standard for *Missional Ministry* and then told His disciples that greater works shall they do. Before He ascended He commanded His disciples to go make disciples and teach them the things that He had taught them.

Modern day outreach is a pathetic shadow of what it used to be in the days of old. There are churches today that boast of the multiplicity of ministries that they have under one roof but sadly, most of those ministries resemble nothing close to biblical evangelism. In most churches, outreach is the most lacking component of all the activities of the church. This should not be.

We must re-think our way of doing Church. Outreach was never intended to be a program within the Church, but the program of the Church. How is it that everyone who followed Jesus, from the 12 disciples to the 70 who were sent out two by two, understood the call of Missional outreach but nobody today feels that they are called or obligated to perform this type of ministry? Has the agenda of God changed?

We have traded in evangelism for marketing, and the results of this transgression has created a generation of believers who feel no spiritual obligation to *Go* into the world and make disciples as the Great Commission has so commanded us to. Our conferences teach us how to build ministries that resemble and operate more like corporations in nature rather than the organic extensions of the Kingdom that the Church was intended to be. *We must Repent.*

How many people in the scriptures do we see get saved while attending a Church service? How many people do we see get saved in the mission field? The answers to these two questions alone should stir up a revival of true evangelistic campaigns within our Churches. It's not that we haven't been winning souls, but there must be a point when we realize that the scriptures have laid out the most effective **blueprint** for winning the lost. It's called evangelism, and this takes place in the mission field, not the Church.

The Evangelist is one of the most misunderstood characters in the Church today. Traditionally we hold the belief that an Evangelist is someone who travels and teaches from Church to Church. This definition falls short of the full role and characteristics necessary to fulfill the duties of someone who walks in the office of an Evangelist.

The Evangelist is one of the most important figures in the mission field. His responsibility is to take on the role of a paramedic, who travels to the trauma scene to perform CPR on those who are clinging to life, or in this case, those in need of spiritual resuscitation. The word Evangelist is defined as *a bringer of good tidings*. The good tidings that he brings are obviously the good news, which we call the Gospel of Jesus Christ.

To evangelize, then, simply means to *preach the Gospel* or *to convert to Christianity*. The secular definition of evangelize is defined as *advocating a cause with the object of making converts*. Without a full understanding of the "biblical" definition of the word evangelize, we naturally feel as if we have been accurately fulfilling these definitions. That's until we dig deeper into the context of the scriptures.

When we think of the word preacher, we automatically draw an image in our minds of someone standing behind a pulpit. This has been our traditional imagery passed down to us of what a preacher is. Unfortunately this limited view has contributed to the minimizing of our ministry efforts over the years.

A preacher in its simplest definition is any blood born again believer who proclaims the Gospel of Jesus or the Kingdom. If you notice Jesus SENT OUT his disciples and told them to preach the Gospel. The purpose of preaching is always intended to lead unbelievers or those living in sin to repentance. The Bible tells us that even Jonah preached to Nineveh a message of repentance and this definitely was not from behind a pulpit.

Culturally, the action of preaching has been viewed as a vocal style of exhortation. When the word *preach* is contrasted against the word *teach* we find how these two words serve to different functions and capacities within ministry. The word preach as stated earlier is defined as the *proclamation of the Gospel* while the word teach is defined as the *installing of doctrine*. Notice that the word *preach* and doctrine are generally never used in association with one another.

Urban Mission Field

You never find Jesus preaching to His disciples, so why do we spend so much time preaching to ours?

The preaching or *proclamation of the Gospel* is something that was intended to generally be done in the mission field through the evangelistic efforts of the Church, while the function of teaching or the *installing of doctrine* is something that was intended to be done in the Church or amongst those who have passed through the gates of repentance unto salvation. Although the proclamation of the Gospel does inherently present a doctrinal announcement, preaching is not the most effective way to present doctrine. That would be the equivalent of attempting to *preach* college algebra.

Preaching is not a tool for discipleship but for repentance. Once salvation has been achieved the believer must be *taught* the disciplines and doctrines of the faith. Culturally, in most urban Churches we spend most of our time preaching. This is why we don't see an abundance of true disciples in our Churches but rather people who are constantly in need of repentance because they have not truly grown in the doctrines of the faith.

We cannot rely on the limited teaching that takes place in Sunday school or some short Discipleship course to make a disciple. We cannot think for one moment that a Sunday morning sermon and mid-week Bible-Study is sufficient in making a disciple. This is why we find people who have been in Church for 40 years and still don't know some of the basic and fundamental doctrines of Christianity. This is why no one in our Churches desires to go into the *Urban Mission Field*.

We must elevate our teaching. The Bible teaches us that our people are "destroyed for a lack of knowledge" (Hosea 4:6). However this same verse goes on to tell us that "because you have rejected knowledge I will reject you from being priest for Me". Many people will reject the knowledge that has just been presented because they do not want to evaluate their traditional viewpoints of ministry.

Just look at the *Urban Mission Field*, it is full of Churches which hold to the traditional viewpoints of ministry and as a result, the communities around them are being destroyed and perishing daily. Churches that are **not** located in the *Urban Mission Field* have overlooked these communities as they outsource their financial contributions to support Global Missions in distant lands and countries. While this is a worthy cause in itself, our first biblical obligation is to preach the Gospel to the surrounding regions and then once that has been fulfilled, to spread the message abroad. Christ did not send His disciples out to the Gentiles first and then tell them to work their way back to the Jews. He told them to start where they were, to spread the Gospel outwards as they labor. After all, charity begins at home.

We've been comforted in the past by the fact that America has been a predominantly Christian nation. Over the past few decades, however, there has been a steep decline in the spiritual composition of America. We are no longer a great "Christian" nation. Some recent surveys show that only approximately 20% of Americans attend church every weekend. Muslim Mosques are popping up faster than Churches in our communities. The Homosexual Community has a greater influence on the direction of our country than the Church.

These statistics should not be fearful but inviting to the Church. It should catch our attention. It allows us to know that there is a beautiful work to be done in the *Urban Mission Field*, and therefore we are to pray to the Lord of the harvest to send out laborers into His harvest (Matthew 9:38). We have to change the way that we think. *We must Repent.*

Chapter Two

Urban Mission Field

2 Timothy 2:2
And the things that you have heard from me among many witnesses, commit these to faithful men who will be able to teach others also.

Pre-Training

Training is one of the most important elements of the evangelical ministry. It is literally one of the main components that undergirds or provides support and strengthens the process of discipleship. The early New Testament Church knew this and made this one of their highest spiritual priorities. They were not motivated by the collection of new members, but by the sending out of converted men back into the field to evangelize the lost with the message of the risen Christ.

The *Urban Mission Field* is a simple but yet complex place to orchestrate effective ministry in. However this by no means gives credence to an excuse to avoid it or continue to put it on the back burner behind all the other activities of the Church. The Urban Mission Field must become the first priority of the Church, and for this to be obtainable, the Church must focus ample time, energy, and resources into training workers to go into the field.

The three main focal points of the church should be worship, discipleship, and evangelism. Each is equally important and is co-dependent on the other. Training is what takes place during discipleship. Our training should lead to evangelism, which is the first part of fulfilling the Great Commission.

A church that fails to perform the Great Commission fails to be a church. This is the reality that most of our churches end up in. Without the proper training the people will never "Go" as Jesus commanded.

> **Matthew 10:7**
> *And as you go, preach, saying, 'The kingdom of heaven is at hand.'*

One of the first things Jesus did after beginning his earthly ministry was to choose for Himself disciples who would be with Him in whom He would personally train and send out into the world to preach. He equipped them with the message to preach. The focus was not on training them to stand behind a pulpit, but on how to make the world their pulpit. One of the problems today is that *our pulpits are too small.*

Our pulpits have become boxed in cages that sit stationary within the four walls of our Churches. We have become trapped and confined in our beautiful cage and the ministry is hindered because we have submitted to our own ways and methods of doing of ministry. If we are going to accomplish results like the early Church achieved, we must follow the pattern that the early Church followed.

Proverbs 14:12
There is a way that seems right to a man, But its end is the way of death.

There are many things that we do in ministry that seem right. Many of these things we do out of a pure and sincere heart. But sincerity of heart does not transform falsehood into fact, and neither does it make the wrong choice a right one. The evidence is that many of our practices in the Church have led to death. One might ask, death where? The answer would be, in our communities. Our communities are dying because we won't *Go*.

Today we consider a mega-church as a church that has 2,000 or more members who attend service on a Sunday morning. These types of ministries take years and even sometimes decades to develop using the current methods commonly practiced within the Church. However, in the Book of Acts the disciples were known to add thousands to the Church in just one day using the methods that Jesus taught them.

One thing for sure is that there is not a sinner shortage in our communities. The harvest is truly great but we must train our people on *how* to work in the *Urban Mission Field*. This takes time and truly takes a changing of thoughts and paradigm due to the traditional approaches of ministry that have been accepted and practiced for so long. Just as Jesus sent out those who followed Him, we must continue in this missional act of sending.

Any time a harvest stays in the field too long it will eventually die. This is what has happened in the Urban Mission Field. No one has been there to harvest the crop so we have suffered catastrophic crop failure due to various environmental factors. Any sustained length of crop failure will eventually lead to famine in the land. This is what we are now seeing in the *Urban Mission Field*.

We must become intentional about training believers for the works of the ministry. This process takes time and dedication. Even more so, it takes individuals who know what it is to serve in this capacity. A disciple can only pour into the next man what has been poured into him.

Most of the training that takes place within the church is focused on training individuals on how to perform various tasks within the premises of the building and within the hours of operation. There is very little training available for missional outreach. Our current models of ministry are not effective at fulfilling the great commission, especially within the Urban Mission Field.

The training to go into any mission field must begin with learning how to proclaim the Gospel. Believe it or not most believers are not equipped to effectively communicate the Gospel. Learning how to proclaim the message does not in any way discredit the fact that one must be Spirit led in every aspect of ministry. However no one can discredit the importance of careful study and preparation.

We have not been preparing our people to *Go,* and since they have not been prepared to *Go,* they *Stay.* We have placed too much emphasis on church activity, concerts, conferences, and festivals, while neglecting missional outreach. There are people who have been sitting on our pews for years who are unequipped for the work that they have been called to do. It comes down to this single fact: we are not doing what Christ asked us to do. *We must Repent.*

Chapter Three

Urban Mission Field

> **Romans 10:9**
> *That if you confess with your mouth, "Jesus is Lord," and believe in your heart that God raised Him from the dead, you will be saved.*

The Roman Road

Jesus equipped His disciples with a message as He sent them out into the world and likewise so should we. What you will find as we survey our churches is that most of the members do not know how to communicate the Gospel. So how can they be sent? We must intentionally train and equip our members to preach and effectively communicate the Gospel.

There are core fundamental aspects of the message that should be present in any presentation of the Gospel. One of the most common methods taught in evangelism is what is called *The Roman Road*. This method is not a script to be used verbatim but a pattern or a good starting point to be used as a template to build upon.

There are a few different variations of this method that exist but once again this method is not at all intended to be the soul-winning script that must be followed.

The Roman Road is basically a compilation of truths used to lead an individual to Christ by using passages that are found in the book of Romans. In essence, the scriptures are used as a "roadmap" to Salvation. As an evangelist, you might never use this approach, but for the purpose of equipping believers on how to proclaim the Gospel, it is a good teaching tool. Nevertheless, without the working of the Holy Spirit, it is just a checklist of scriptures.

Attempting to witness to someone can in no way be accomplished in the flesh. When we attempt things in the flesh we get results of the flesh. When we attempt things in the Spirit we get results of the Spirit. We must pray that the Holy Spirit is in control of every aspect of our witnessing.

Once again, *The Roman Road* is only a template and not intended to be used as script unto Salvation. It is a good teaching tool for equipping believers, but in reality we cannot treat our soul-winning efforts like a step-by-step assembly line process. Each person may lead an unbeliever to Christ in whatever way he or she is led by the Holy Spirit to do so. There is no one-way or specific prayer that must be spoken, but there is only one message, which is the Gospel of Jesus Christ.

If a minister is going to be successful in winning souls, he must be convinced and saturated with this message himself. You cannot merely remember some scriptures and principles and expect to be used by God. One can learn methodologies of soul-winning but until he has had a Damascus road type experience, he will be no more effective at winning souls than a robot that has been programmed to speak but yet lacks the ability to discern and the ability to clearly hear the voice of the Holy Spirit.

2 Corinthians 7:10
For godly sorrow worketh repentance to salvation not to be repented of: but the sorrow of the world worketh death.

So many times we see ministers stand before crowds of people and have them repeat a cookie cutter prayer followed by the blasphemous lie that they have all received salvation. Ministers will brag on how many people repeated a simple prayer. However, there is no salvation without repentance. And just as the works of the flesh are evident, so much more evident are the fruits of repentance. Jesus said "There is joy in the presence of the angels of God over one sinner who repents" (Luke 15:10). The joy is not over them repeating a prayer, but their sincere act of repentance.

As such, we must not attempt to rush or push a person into saying a prayer or signing a decision card. These tactics do more harm than good. Our churches are full of forged decision cards of people who have never touched the altar of repentance. Our membership books are polluted with the names of people who are no more saved than a Buddhist Monk who has denied Christ and chosen not to believe the Gospel of truth.

The key point is that the individual must realize that they are a sinner in need of a Savior, and you cannot convince them of that by carnal or natural means. It takes an individual filled and led by the Holy Spirit to deliver this type of conviction. Salvation is a supernatural work of God that cannot be accomplished through the reasoning of man. It cannot be done without the Gospel, for it is the power of God unto salvation (Romans 1:16).

Before a person will seek or request a cure, they must come to the realization that they are sick. The reason most attempts to lead someone to Christ fail is because the unbeliever fails to realize the spiritual state of their soul because we, as evangelists, have failed to communicate the Gospel. So there is no brokenness and no repentance. Without repentance, there can be no salvation.

Most people in their own mind already feel that they have salvation just because they believe that God exists. However, the scriptures teach us that even the demons believe and tremble (James 2:19). God is not just looking for someone who will simply believe that He exists, but someone whose beliefs cause them to become a follower of Christ, and it takes more than repeating a prayer. **We cannot afford to make false converts.** *We must Repent.*

Chapter Four

Isaiah 55:11
So shall My word be that goes forth from My mouth; It shall not return to Me void, But it shall accomplish what I please, And it shall prosper in the thing for which I sent it.

What Next

It is a realistic expectation that when we enter the *Urban Mission Field*, souls will be saved. When the Gospel is preached to unconverted men, the Gospel will do what it has been sent to do. It shall not return void. But what happens after the prayer? What next?

Once you have successfully led someone to Christ, it is of extreme importance that you get his or her contact information if you have not already done so. The next few weeks that follow their decision will be the most important time period in their new life. Remember you have just entered them into a war and they now have a target on their back in the spirit realm. It is now the responsibility of the ministry to make sure that they get into a position where they can be "discipled".

Discipleship is the point. The Great Commission commands us to go and make disciples, but many times we stop at the point of Salvation, leaving the new convert ill-equipped for the battle into which they have just been enlisted. What usually happens after this is the new convert becomes non-responsive to the call of ministry that is on their lives. This is one of the greatest tragedies that we see today in our outreach efforts.

Preparation is one of the most important elements when going into the *Urban Mission Field*. If at all possible, you should have some type of material to place in the hand of a new convert before you walk away. This is also useful for those who may have rejected your efforts and for those who might be in a backslidden state of their walk with Jesus. This material can be a DVD, CD, business card, flyer, or any other type of Christian publication. It is usually best if the material is relevant to the person that you have witnessed to. For the new convert, this will help them in further understanding the decision that they have just made.

A large percentage of new converts fall right back into sin shortly after their conversion experience because there is no one there to walk with them along the way. No man can disciple himself. With this understanding it becomes essential that before we begin evangelism in the *Urban Mission Field,* that the ministry must have people set in place who can make disciples of new converts. A man can only pour into the next man what's been poured into him. The biggest mistake made in evangelism is leading someone to Christ and never getting back with them.

Matthew 13:19
When anyone hears the word of the kingdom, and does not understand it, then the wicked one comes and snatches away what was sown in his heart. This is he who received seed by the wayside.

Jesus tells us "When anyone hears the word of the kingdom, and does not understand *it*, then the wicked *one* comes and snatches away what was sown in his heart." Every minister must understand that the enemy is only one step behind us looking to snatch up everything that we sow before it can take root and grow. While the minister is busy bragging about how many prayed a scripted prayer or received what they perceived to be salvation, Satan is busy attempting to snatch up the word that was sown in their hearts.

Luke 8:12
Those by the wayside are the ones who hear; then the devil comes and takes away the word out of their hearts, lest they should believe and be saved.

So many times we allow the word to be aborted because we feel that we have sown a seed. We find justification in our lack of commitment to the work by pointing to the small things that we have done. We must be persistent and follow through with every work that we begin. It is not enough to just throw seeds, but we must plant, and plant with the understanding that our *"adversary the devil walks about like a roaring lion, seeking whom he may devour"* (1 Peter 5:8).

We throw seeds at the soil of the hearts of men and run while claiming that a seed was planted. If you didn't plant, most likely that seed was snatched. We are so careless in our evangelism-witnessing efforts. We have come up with so many clever techniques and methods of *witnessing* without actually *witnessing* that most of what we do can no longer be classified as *witnessing*.

We must understand that Satan has been doing what he does for thousands of years, while we have only been doing what we do for a few years, decades at best. The enemy knows that without discipleship that a new convert will quickly slip back into the bondage of sin that he was rescued from. Remember, we were commanded to **"Make Disciples"**, not just lead unbelievers in prayer. We must see the bigger picture.

Urban Mission Field

Contrary to popular thought, a disciple cannot be made on Sunday Morning. It is a drawn out process that takes time and dedication. Look at how much time Jesus spent with His disciples. The art of discipleship has been lost over the generations. Jesus took a small group of ordinary people and trained them to do extraordinary works. We must revive the ways of old and return to the way of the Master. *We must Repent.*

Chapter Five

> **1 Corinthians 9:19**
> *For though I am free from all men, I have made myself a servant to all, that I might win the more;* [20] *and to the Jews I became as a Jew, that I might win Jews; to those who are under the law, as under the law, that I might win those who are under the law;* [21] *to those who are without law, as without law (not being without law toward God, but under law toward Christ), that I might win those who are without law;* [22] *to the weak I became as weak, that I might win the weak. I have become all things to all men, that I might by all means save some.*

Becoming All Things

If we are to become effective in the *Urban Mission Field*, we must learn to become a bridge to all men. Before a missionary goes into a foreign mission field, he seeks first to understand the culture and the language of the people group in which he has been sent to. One of his most important objectives is effective communication because he knows that he must communicate the message of the Gospel to a foreign people.

The *Urban Mission Field* is no different than the foreign mission field. There are many cultural barriers that must be crossed on the way to sharing the Gospel. The lingo of the church is like a foreign language to those who are not a part of the church culture. Many times we are rejected not because of the Gospel, but because of our inability to communicate it in a relative manner.

One of the most common things we see in many of our churches is the absorption of tradition amongst those who serve in ministry. We assume that when we obtain a certain set of words and adapt to a certain way of saying them that we then become effective as ministers. It's almost as if it's an unspoken rule that if a minister doesn't look or speak a certain way, then he is not a minister. What most will find is that what works in the church does not work in the *Urban Mission Field*.

Sometimes the odor of our traditional jargon will push the unbeliever away, especially those who are within the *Urban Mission Field*. We must understand that many people are running from this very manifestation of traditionalism and ritualism which masquerades as if it were the church in many of our communities. This is what pushes and repels many away from the church. It's not that they have run from the church, it's that they have run from what they have seen which was called the church, but was no more than traditions and dead rituals in a box.

What is needed is true genuineness. When we enter the *Urban Mission Field* we must leave the church at the church and be the Church. In other words we must not bring our traditional mindset with us. Simply stated, we must be real. We are trying to reach a foreign people group. The three-piece suits, Stacy Adam's shoes, the choir robes, the collars, all of these things will do nothing more than work against us in the field.

The people must see Christ Jesus in us. They must see nothing but the compassion of God and not an ounce of self-righteousness or we will utterly fail. We must not become judgmental, while at the same time we cannot conform or dilute the Gospel in any manner. The balance of not being judgmental while maintaining the potency of the Gospel is paramount in the field. It is extremely easy for any man to fall into a judgmental and self-righteousness state of mind.

> **Matthew 9:10**
> *Now it happened, as Jesus sat at the table in the house, that behold, many tax collectors and sinners came and sat down with Him and His disciples. [11] And when the Pharisees saw it, they said to His disciples, "Why does your Teacher eat with tax collectors and sinners?"*

Jesus made it a point to be amongst the sinners, and they welcomed Him. We find Him in the Gospels sitting down and eating with tax collectors and sinners. In Jewish culture, tax collectors were considered to be the outcast of the society, for they worked for the Roman Empire which had basically conquered the Jews. The tax collectors did just that, collect taxes, and they were hated by their countrymen because they collected more taxes than was due and kept the excess for themselves. The Pharisees even questioned why Jesus was eating with the tax collectors and sinners. But what better place to be than amongst sinners if your intention is to preach the Gospel and save souls?

The sinners are the people that we have been called to reach. Notice how Jesus would sit down and eat with them. What better way to show compassion and genuineness than to sit down amongst sinners and break bread? They were drawn to Him. Jesus wasn't trying to invite them to a church service or a concert, but He would talk to them about things concerning the Kingdom of God.

We have to accept the fact that the lost are not volunteering to come to our churches. This is why we must bring the church to them. Not the tradition of the church, but the true manifestation of the church. We must be prepared to begin discipleship in their place of comfort for a season. As they begin to grow in the faith, they will become more open to follow us to our place of worship.

The bottom line is that people will respond to the message of the Gospel when it is presented to them properly. As ministers of the Gospel in the field we must be engaging. We must learn how to talk to and with people and not at them. Mission Field etiquette is essential. We are not required to be great men and women of speech with eloquent articulation, but we must excel in people skills.

1 Corinthians 1:18
For the preaching of the cross is to them that perish foolishness; but unto us which are saved it is the power of God.

So many people have been turned away from the church because of someone who may have come with the right message came at them the wrong way. The Gospel itself is foolishness to them who are perishing, so we need not hinder the message through our ignorance and lack of people skills. Understanding how to become all things to all men will take us very far in the *Urban Mission Field*.

We must also understand how to witness to people of other faiths. So many time Christians will shy away at the opportunity to share their faith with somebody who is of another religion. Why is this? Are we not called for this very work? Do people of other religions not fall under the grand umbrella of The Great Commission, or is salvation available only to those who come from Christian households?

The reality is that our communities are becoming more and more diverse in culture, faith, and religion. Muslim Mosques and Buddhist Temples are being built faster than churches in some areas. Unfortunately many of our churches have adapted a postmodern train of thought. We seek to co-exist with other religions instead of praying for their conversion. We join in interfaith projects and seek self-preservation instead of being intentional and radical about evangelizing.

Urban Mission Field

In the Book of Acts (17:16-35) the Apostle Paul was stirred in his spirit when he saw the city of Athens given wholly to idolatry. Are we not so stirred in our spirit to see our communities and mission fields given to idolatry? Do we even pay attention to such things? Do we walk into their temples and preach Christ? Until we come to the conclusion that every religion & doctrine outside of Christ Jesus is idolatry and the worship of demons, we will never be moved in such a way.

> **1 Corinthians 10:20**
> *Rather, that the things which the Gentiles sacrifice they sacrifice to demons and not to God, and I do not want you to have fellowship with demons.*

There is no self-preservation in Christ. How many countless souls of other faiths will perish in Hell because no one was bold enough or compassionate enough to share with them *The Way* which is only found in Christ Jesus? We must truly become all things to all men so that by all means we might save some. We must make it our goal to reach the Muslim, the Buddhist, the Hindu, the Jehovah's Witness, the Mormon, the Wiccan, the Catholic, the atheist, the Homosexual, and all those who are lost. *We must Repent.*

Chapter Six

Urban Mission Field

Acts 1:8
But you shall receive power when the Holy Spirit has come upon you; and you shall be witnesses to Me in Jerusalem, and in all Judea and Samaria, and to the end of the earth."

Witnessing

The act of witnessing should be one of the highest spiritual priorities of any believer. It is the one spiritual gift that we should all share in common. The Bible teaches that a believer who is filled with the Holy Spirit shall be a witness. Jesus told His disciples shortly before He ascended that they would receive power when the Holy Spirit comes upon them, and that they shall be witness to Him. Technically, witnessing should come easy because it is not of the flesh but through the power of the Holy Spirit. Why then do we have so few witnesses?

We have become so consumed with the desire for titles and positions that we have neglected the primary position, the position of a witness. Isn't it interesting that after years of theological debate that we still struggle in figuring out what roles most of the individuals mentioned in the New Testament served within the Church? The only thing that they were concerned with is witnessing.

To be called as a witness is a privilege. A witness is someone who has seen, heard, or experienced and is willing to testify of the evidence they have encountered. For the believer, our court is the world and we are trying to convince the jury to make a decision of faith based on the evidence that we have presented to them. Oh how many people plead the 5th or fail to show up to court to testify.

> **2 Corinthians 5:11**
> *Knowing, therefore, the terror of the Lord, we persuade men; but we are well known to God, and I also trust are well known in your consciences.*

When one obtains a true understanding of the terror of the Lord he will not be able to restrain himself from witnessing. He will understand that without Christ, all are without hope and on a direct collision coarse with Hell. He will begin to persuade men to repent of their sins unto Salvation. He will be a witness.

We must ask God for compassion for His people. If you are ever going to be effective in the *Urban Mission Field* you must have a God-born zeal to reach and restore people who are lost and in need of the Gospel of Jesus Christ. Until this happens, your witnessing will not be effective. You will burn out quickly because the flesh can never accomplish the works of the Spirit. This is why many people do not do this type of ministry.

Hundreds of people will line up to preach behind a wooden pulpit, but not many would be willing to take the message of Christ to the world and stare unconverted men in the eyes and proclaim to them that they must repent. Flesh could never desire the ways of God.

Many of the ministries in what the 21st century Church has become can be accomplished in the flesh without anyone discerning the difference. It has become obvious that people can achieve "superficial" success in their ministries without tapping into the power of the Holy Spirit. For example, many musicians get by with natural talent without ever tapping into the anointing. Many preachers preach sermons without a word from the Holy Spirit. Sadly, many churches prosper in numbers that God has never visited.

It becomes evident that the anointing is absent when we see people come and participate in our services over and over and leave still entangled in the bondage of sin. The absence of such anointing becomes even more apparent when we see ministers stand before the people and yet they still walk in the most perversion of sin. Are we satisfied with such results? Are we satisfied with people just paying attention to us speak giving us a reaction when we raise our voice to the tune of the organ? There has to be more.

The anointing destroys the yoke. There is no way that we can enter into the presence of God and leave the same. If we desire to be great soul winners for God we must deal with **sin** in the camp. Sin will stand between you and God as a wall of separation stands between a man and a desired path (Isaiah 59:2). Sin will quench the very fire of the Holy Spirit in our lives. Sin will hinder us from being a witness.

On the contrary, the evidence of a true Holy Spirit filled believer is that he will become a witness. This truth is not fulfilled in the casual conversation of God. This truth is not confirmed through the mentioning of religious beliefs. This truth is exclusively lived out through the intentional proclamation of the Gospel with the anticipated goal of leading a soul to Christ.

We have watered the act of witnessing down to such a degree that it is barely detectable when we attempt to do it. We justify this delusion by insisting that we do not want to offend anyone as if the Gospel is not a non-offensive exclusive message already. Through our act of claiming not to want to offend anyone, we willingly sacrifice so many souls because we reserve the fullness of the message of the Gospel. This is not the work of the Holy Spirit.

Jeremiah 26:2
Thus saith the LORD; Stand in the court of the LORD's house, and speak unto all the cities of Judah, which come to worship in the LORD's house, all the words that I command thee to speak unto them; diminish not a word

We can by no means diminish the word of God and expect the results that we read about in the scriptures. There is not one scripture that justifies such actions. Whether we are in the Lord's house or in the mission field, we must speak every word that He has commanded us to speak. Watered down medicine is not effective.

We must witness and share the Gospel with the understanding and conviction that the people of the world depend on it. We must revive the old paths and return to the ways of the Master. We must see the depravity of mankind and respond with the only message that can save a soul. We must preach the Gospel of Jesus Christ until transformation takes place in the land. We must recognize our error and our own transgressions. *We must Repent.*

Chapter Seven

Psalm 62:5
My soul, wait silently for God alone, for my expectation is from Him.

Expectation

We must stop settling for anything short of a supernatural experience when we come together and serve in His name. Beautiful things happen when the Gospel is proclaimed and the Kingdom of God is announced in the atmosphere. Spiritual principalities and the powers of darkness flee, the captives are set free, and miraculous signs and wonders follow.

Since this is all scriptural, why shouldn't we expect these things to come to pass when we fulfill our duty? Expectation is the backbone of faith. Our faith is the expectation that God is going to do something, the undeniable reality that God, who cannot fail, is going to confirm His word.

Every time we enter the mission field we should expect for God to do something magnificent. Remember He said that as we *GO*, that He would be with us. We are called as co-laborers, laboring in the field with Christ Himself. We should expect nothing short of a supernatural experience every time we step foot onto the mission field with Jesus. If we don't expect anyone to come to faith, then no one will. If we don't expect the masses to respond to the message we are bringing, they will not, because our doubt will contaminate our message as we stand as witnesses to testify to the jury.

> **2 Timothy 1:7**
> *For God hath not given us the spirit of fear; but of power, and of love, and of a sound mind.*

Most people refrain from witnessing because of fear. Fear is a spirit that God has NOT given to us, so it must be dealt with if you plan on being effective in the *Urban Mission Field*. Fear and Expectation cannot co-exist together. So many times people allow fear to hinder them from sharing Christ with a person in dire need of the Gospel. How can we see someone who we know is living outside of the will of God and not witness to them?

Fear will absolutely paralyze you from witnessing. Fear will block the expectation of God doing something and render you useless in the field. Our enemy the devil does not want us to be effective in witnessing so therefore he will attempt to use fear to accomplish his goal. When we stand before the people, he will attempt to tell us that we have not the words to reach them. But oh we do!

If we truly believed the message that we preached, then through our faith we would have the expectation of faith that repentance would follow whenever we witness to the lost. The Gospel is the most majestic and powerful message under the sun. Countless numbers of souls have been saved by this message alone, a message that has been entrusted to us. Without expectation and action, we will never see results of the Gospel of Jesus Christ in the *Urban Mission Field*. Shouldn't we desire the same results that we read about in the scriptures?

> **Matthew 15:6**
> *Thus you have made the commandment of God of no effect by your tradition*

The Word of God tells us to *GO* into the world and make disciples. Our tradition tells us to stay in the building and make members. The Word of God tells us that certain signs should follow those who walk in the Great Commission. Our tradition in many churches tells us that these signs have ceased to exist. In the areas where the Word of God and our traditions contradict one another, we make the commandment of God of no effect.

We must be willing to let go of all of the traditional baggage that we carry in our churches. Our traditions, which are not rooted in sound doctrine, have the power to make the word of God of no effect in our churches. We can no longer continue to do ministry the way that we want to and expect the results that the Word of God says that we should see.

If a man with no vehicle walked into a car dealership with A1 credit and a bag of money, the salesmen would be jumping over tables trying to get to him to make a sale. It would be understood that based on his needs, outstanding credit, and his cash that this man was in great position and pre-qualified to purchase a vehicle. The salesman would be 100% confident that a deal would be closed. He would have great expectations of success.

How much more expectation than a car salesman in the best position to make a sale should a man of God that is equipped with the Gospel of Jesus Christ have? Every person that we stand in front of is all ready pre-qualified for salvation. They need this message to get where they need to go, and the best part about it is that it's FREE. No money down, no payments, no interest, just a DECISION… **REPENT** and live. *We must Repent.*

Chapter Eight

Urban Mission Field

> **2 Corinthians 5:20**
> *Now then, we are ambassadors for Christ, as though God were pleading through us: we implore you on Christ's behalf, be reconciled to God.*

God's Workers

One of the most beautiful aspects of our walk is that we have been called to this work by the God and creator of the Universe. We are called to be ambassadors for Christ. An ambassador, as the highest ranking diplomat who represents a nation or kingdom in a foreign land, is a person who is entrusted with immense responsibility. When you consider that we, as ambassadors for Christ, are being called not to represent some earthly kingdom but the timeless, unending and unconquerable Kingdom of God, the concept is almost overwhelming. We have been called to stand in representation of Christ on behalf of the Kingdom of God in this foreign land. What greater call is there?

God uses us to speak to the nations and to those who are in sin. He desires the reconciliation of man back to Himself and He uses us to proclaim the only message that can accomplish this. Every time God has us to share our faith with someone, God is pleading with them through us (2 Corinthians 5:20). He loves us so much that He pleads with us to come back to Him.

To be used by God is an honor and a privilege that cannot be taken for granted, considering that we are not even worthy to speak of His name or to be in His presence. Nonetheless, He still chooses to use us. Rather than answer to this call, many people choose to minimize what the scripture has commanded and rationalize the meaning until there is no substance remaining.

2 Corinthians 10:15-16
not boasting of things beyond measure, that is, in other men's labors, but having hope, that as your faith is increased, we shall be greatly enlarged by you in our sphere, 16 to preach the gospel in the regions beyond you, and not to boast in another man's sphere of accomplishment.

What employee gets a paycheck for another man's labor? How long will a company pay a man who never does the work that has been assigned to him? This is not multi-level marketing. There is no boast in another man's sphere of accomplishment. We must do this work. We must preach the Gospel.

To our own shame *Jehovah Witnesses* and *Mormons* have better evangelism discipline than the true Church which descends from the Church of old. They are adamant and consistent about sharing their message. They are doing what we have been called to do and while we sit back and laugh at their practices, thousands of people are being indoctrinated with a **false Gospel**. This is not funny.

We are bondservants to this Gospel and we must stop conducting business as usual. The men written about in the scriptures would not fit into our brand of Christianity. They would be radically different and seem to be overly aggressive in their approach to doing ministry. They would be ostracized from our seminaries and not welcomed to our conferences. They would be shunned from our churches and not received in our associations. Many would say that they took the Bible too literally. Well isn't that the point? Shouldn't men say that we take the Bible too literally? When will we once again start taking the Bible literally?

The men of old were so indebted to the Gospel that they considered themselves bondservants. A bondservant has no choice; he is bound to the work of his master because he has been bought. When we chose the gift of Salvation we chose to give up our life in exchange for LIFE. *It is no longer I who lives, but Christ lives in us* (Galatians 2:20). We have been bought for a price and crucified with Christ. Our purpose is found in serving the King. God does not save people just to have them sit on a pew. Each and every one of us fit intricately into God's ultimate plan for the redemption of mankind.

Christ paid the ultimate price for us when He died on the cross. What He expects from us, and what is required of every Christian, is that we participate in His work of redemption by preaching AND living His word. If a bank was giving away money we would be quick, even on fire, to share this information with our friends, neighbors and co-workers. When it comes to the Gospel, the very message that will determine the eternal fate of our souls, we are hesitant to share such news. This attitude has nearly cost us a generation.

It is one thing to preach the Gospel from behind a pulpit, but it is a totally different work to share the Gospel in the mission field. Fear will attempt to stand as an obstacle preventing you from reaching the level of communication needed to connect. But this is the true call. We have this one simple call: **Go!** The moment we begin to stand still we stand in direct disobedience to the call of the New Testament Church.

Even in our most sincere attempts to lead someone to Christ we must be conscious and discerning on how we communicate the Gospel. First we must be careful that it is the Gospel that we are communicating. There are many who use unscriptural methods and techniques in their evangelical attempts. The only message that will and can save a soul is the Gospel of Jesus Christ.

We must be careful not to use fear as a means of pushing someone towards making a decision or saying a prayer. If all you do is illustrate and push a message of hell in your evangelistic efforts you will not be successful at soul winning. Even a snake has enough sense to run from fire but at the end of the day he is still a snake. What we are attempting to do is to change the *nature* of the snake through the Word of God, not just to make it aware of the danger of fire. This is not to say that converts will not be in fear of the Lord as they are convicted from the message of Gospel, but the issue is they must turn away from a their sin, and that is what He came to save us from (Matthew 1:21)

Fear and ignorance are the dominant ingredients in making a false convert. A little bit of fear mixed with a little bit of ignorance and you have just successfully created a false convert. These types of converts will either quickly walk away from their decision or rest in the self-justified status of believing that they are saved when truly there has been no repentance. True conversion calls for a change of direction, a moving away from sin that is reflected in the choices we make, the friends we have, and the activities we indulge in. The fear of hell may get someone's attention, but it is not strong enough to bring about a change of heart. The fear of hell and the fear of the Lord are two different things not to be mistaken.

Luke 6:46
And why call ye me, Lord, Lord, and do not the things which I say?

A majority of self-professing Christians are no more than false converts. As judgmental as this may sound, even Jesus said

Urban Mission Field

"narrow is the gate and difficult is the way which leads to life, and there are few who find it" (Mt 7:14). It's not an easy path and those who proclaim the Gospel have one of the most critical responsibilities that a man could ever have. It is our responsibility and privilege to proclaim the Gospel of Jesus Christ to the lost. We must take our rightful abode. *We must Repent.*

Chapter Nine

Proverbs 14:12
There is a way that seems right to a man, But its end is the way of death.

The Blueprint

Over the past few decades there have been many books, techniques, and methods that have surfaced on witnessing and sharing one's faith. As great as some of these methods may seem, most of them are truly ineffective at soul winning. The evidence can be seen in the lack of new converts being brought in from outside of the Church.

21st century Christianity has major advantages over the early Church in the areas of technology, communications, knowledge of the world, and transportation. However, 1st century Christianity was far superior in its effectiveness in spreading the Gospel and displaying the power of God. How often can we truly say that we resemble the early Church, if at all?

Christians have adopted such a passive, non-aggressive approach to witnessing that it no longer should be labeled evangelism. Where is the power that Jesus spoke of? Where is the boldness that we see in the book of Acts? How can we be satisfied with the results that we get? We must take a closer look at our approach to ministry and compare it to what we see in scripture.

Jesus laid out in the Gospels the **blueprint** for evangelism. With much labor, He trained His disciples on how to effectively reach the lost. He sat them down day after day and taught them. He led by example and He frequently sent them out to do the work of the ministry. He showed them what ministry looked like and groomed them to fulfill it.

Jesus did not meet with his disciples once a week on Sunday morning and stand behind a pulpit to give them three points and a closing. He invited them to observe His life and His walk. They learned how to follow Him and learned how to imitate Him. He did not keep them sheltered inside of some building teaching them twelve principles to financial security. Jesus lived His ministry, in the mission field, and His life itself was a lesson in discipleship for those who followed Him. If we were to adopt this discipline, then we would be talking less and showing more by the way walk.

Do we not get it? God wants us to do the work. If He didn't, Jesus would have never trained His disciples in such a manner. They set the standard for ministry. We were not given the accounts of their works for enjoyment and storytelling time, but for instruction unto righteousness.

Most of Jesus' documented ministry was spent outside ministering to the people, healing the sick, and reaching the lost. It is no coincidence that after His resurrection that He gave His disciples what we have come to know as the Great Commission, a **blueprint** or instructions on what we are to do.

Matthew 28:18-20
"All authority has been given to Me in heaven and on earth. [19] Go therefore and make disciples of all the nations, baptizing them in the name of the Father and of the Son and of the Holy Spirit, [20] teaching them to observe all things that I have commanded you; and lo, I am with you always, even to the end of the age."

Mark 16:15-18
"Go into all the world and preach the gospel to every creature. [16] He who believes and is baptized will be saved; but he who does not believe will be condemned. [17] And these signs will follow those who believe: In My name they will cast out demons; they will speak with new tongues; [18] they will take up serpents; and if they drink anything deadly, it will by no means hurt them; they will lay hands on the sick, and they will recover."

The Great Commission is such a simple but yet profound proclamation that Jesus charged to His disciples. Jesus did not make a request, but a command for His disciples to *"Go"* into the world. He did not stop at *Go*, but He told them what to do and what should follow. He told them what the evidence would be as they fulfilled this command. But we no longer want to *Go*. We expect them (the lost) to come.

The fact that we will no longer *Go* is the reason why we have so much darkness in our land today. This is why the communities in which our churches inhabit have such an abundance of crime and nearly every evil thing under the sun. This is why our churches have no dominion over the land.

We have compromised our great call and laid down our authority and the enemy has been having a field day in our communities. Instead of following the simple **blueprint** that was given to us, we have drawn up our own plans. God has not called us to figure out how to redeem the lost, He has already revealed it to us. He has called us to follow His lead. We have chosen instead to go our own way as if we know where to go.

Acts 16:5
So the churches were strengthened in the faith, and increased in number daily.

In the book of Acts we see the early church following the same **blueprint** that Jesus laid out. The results were beautiful. The evidence that Jesus spoke of clearly followed them. The church grew by leaps and bounds with new converts to the faith, not church transfers or those born into Christian households, but new converts. We must return to the blueprint given to us.

The early church expressed such an extreme urgency to fulfill the great commission. They followed the **blueprint** to perfection. They were so missional in their way of thinking that they embodied the very call of ministry in their lives. They lived it out. It was simply who they were. There was no duality of self or balancing their life as a minister and a man. They knew that they were brought together for this work.

Matthew 7:21-23
"Not everyone who says to Me, 'Lord, Lord,' shall enter the kingdom of heaven, but he who does the will of My Father in heaven ²² Many will say to Me in that day, 'Lord, Lord, have we not prophesied in Your name, cast out demons in Your name, and done many wonders in Your name?' ²³ And then I will declare to them 'I never knew you; depart from Me, you who practice lawlessness!'

We feel that our activities justify our walk when in actuality they do not. Jesus said that "he who does the will" of the Father shall enter the Kingdom of Heaven. The will of the Father is fully embodied in the **blueprint** that was given unto us is to make disciples. That's what He taught us, that's what His disciples observed from Him.

Urban Mission Field

Notice how the people spoken of in Matthew 7:22 will try on "that day" to justify their walk by pointing to their activities, stating that they have prophesied, cast out demons, and done many wonders in His name. Jesus said these signs should follow us as we *"Go"*, and He commanded us to make disciples. Which brings us to the point that we can have all the activity, all the signs and wonders, but if we did not make disciples, then we did not do the will of the Father. *We must Repent.*

Chapter Ten

Mark 1:17
Then Jesus said to them, "Follow Me, and I will make you become fishers of men."

Fisher Of Men

To be a Christian is to be a follower of Christ. But what exactly does this look like? Jesus said, "Follow Me, and I will make you become fishers of men". The true litmus test of Christianity, then, is if we are transformed into fishers of men. This is the goal of discipleship, that through the ever-growing relationship with Christ and the study of the word that one will become a fisher of men.

In the natural, a fisherman will find a place that is abundant in fish to cast his net in. It would not make sense for him to cast his net upon a tree or anywhere on dry land, because that is not where fish reside. He would never catch any fish with such ignorant practices.

However, through training and real life application, a fisherman will learn the best times and locations to fish, as well as various techniques for casting his net and hauling in his catch. He would gain the understanding of how fish react and the best types of baits to use to attract them. If he were to be productive in his craft and if this were what he lived by, by all means he would fish. Why do we not fish?

> **John 12:26**
> *If anyone serves Me, let him follow Me; and where I am, there My servant will be also.*

How is it that one can claim to be a Christian and never cast a net into the water? How is that one can claim to be a disciple and never even go into the water? How is it that one can claim to be a follower of someone he never follows? Jesus said, "where I am, there my servant will be also", but we want Him to be where we are. We want Him to follow us. We must remember that He has invited us to follow Him.

Where do we usually find Jesus in the Gospels? In the mission field, ministering to the lost and broken. If Jesus were here today where would we find Him? We would find Him in the most broken and deprived communities praying and laying hands on the sick, preaching and reaching the lost, leading and grooming disciples. This is exactly where we should be found. How can we claim to follow Him when we know not this type of work? *We must Repent.*

Jesus told His disciples to make disciples, not Christians. It was the world that looked at the Disciples in the book of Acts in Antioch and labeled them Christians (Acts 11:26). You see they saw a people who looked so much like Christ, who walked so much like Christ, and lived so much like Christ that they branded them Christians, hence followers of Christ.

Our lives should reflect so much of the incarnation of Christ that those in the world would look upon us and know that we are following Jesus. Just because one studies the Bible does not mean that he follows Jesus. Do you think that the life of the early Church was merely the study of the word and Church service? No, it was living out the word as fishers of men.

> **Acts 4:13**
> *Now when they saw the boldness of Peter and John, and perceived that they were uneducated and untrained men, they marveled. And they realized that they had been with Jesus.*

When a believer has been with Jesus it is evident. Not only will his words testify of Him, but also his life will testify. Bystanders will see Christ in him and glorify God. Those who are not of the faith will look upon him and marvel. When was the last time the world realized that you had been with Jesus? Does the world even know that you are following Jesus?

To be a fisher of men is to be a follower of Christ. This is His goal for our lives, His plan for growing His Church and His model of discipleship and outreach. Why won't we fish? How can we be satisfied with the occasional fish that finds his or her way to our dry land? How can we be satisfied with fish that come from another aquarium or church as if we've done some great work?

> **1 John 2:6**
> *He who says he abides in Him ought himself also to walk just as He walked.*

We have not only been called to believe in Him who was slain for the sins of the world, but also to walk as He walked. When we look at the footprints that Christ left in the sand they are very detailed and easy to follow. As believers, we must strive to walk just as He walked and through humility and the fear of God, we must swiftly correct our paths when they do not line up with the steps that He has laid before us.

Anybody can claim to be a Christian, but not everyone can declare to be a disciple. A disciple will be found to be where Jesus is, amongst the lost. A disciple will be ridiculed for eating with the thugs, gangsters, and criminals, who are the tax-collector type people-group of the present day. A disciple will be found with a net in his hand pulling in fish from the water. A disciple will be found fishing.

Philippians 2:5
Let this mind be in you which was also in Christ Jesus

We must take on the same mindset as Christ Jesus. When we read the Gospels it becomes vividly apparent that the mind of Jesus was extremely missional in purpose. Jesus was the greatest missionary of all time, a fisher of men. How can we claim to have this mind, and not fish?

The average Christian will go through his entire life without ever pulling one fish out of the water. We have distorted ministry to such a point that it is almost no longer recognizable by even the most trained eye. How is it possible to read the Gospels and the Book of Acts and still feel any ancestral relationship between what we read and the spiritual disciplines that we practice? *We must Repent.*

Chapter Eleven

Proverbs 11:30
The fruit of the righteous is a tree of life, and he who wins souls is wise.

What Time Is It?

It is 11:30, time to win souls. Proverbs 11:30 proclaims that he who wins souls is wise. Simply stated, a wise man wins souls. The fruit that comes from the righteous is a tree of life. Evangelism is all about winning souls. When we step out onto the *urban mission field* it is 11:30, time to win souls. We should strive for nothing less.

Why do we expect gentiles to find their way to the church? We are so impressed with what was taught at the last church growth seminar that we have forsaken the way of the master for an easier less life-consuming route. There are souls that hang in the balance everyday while we have become content with playing church. We cannot expect for gentiles to desire righteousness.

Ezekiel 3:17-19
"Son of man, I have made you a watchman for the house of Israel; therefore hear a word from My mouth, and give them warning from Me: 18 When I say to the wicked, 'You shall surely die,' and you give him no warning, nor speak to warn the wicked from his wicked way, to save his life, that same wicked man shall die in his iniquity; but his blood I will require at your hand. 19 Yet, if you warn the wicked, and he does not turn from his wickedness, nor from his wicked way, he shall die in his iniquity; but you have delivered your soul.

God has put a message of repentance into our mouths and commissioned us to *Go* into the world and make disciples, but we won't *Go*. We will not *Go* and warn the wicked of his wicked ways. We will not *Go* to save his life which is far more valuable than the resources that we seek after on a consistent basis for our ministries. Do you not know how much blood is on our hands?

If you saw a child drowning would you not jump in to save his life? If you saw an elderly man about to get hit by a bus would you not do everything in your power to save his life? Have we stopped to consider the value of the soul of a man? Why will we not *Go*? Why will we not *Go* into the world with this message of repentance that God has put into our mouths and warn the wicked that *"you shall surely die"*?

We have been disobedient to the call of God. Our disobedience has not only hurt others, but it places our very souls in danger. Do you not know that when we fulfill the call that we not only deliver others, but that we deliver our own souls (Ezekiel 3:19)? He who wins souls is wise.

2 Corinthians 5:18, 19
Now all things are of God, who has reconciled us to Himself through Jesus Christ, and has given us the ministry of reconciliation, 19 that is, that God

> *was in Christ reconciling the world to Himself, not imputing their trespasses to them, and has committed to us the word of reconciliation.*

Every time we enter the *Urban Mission Field* we must enter with the understanding that we have been sent by God on an assignment. Our train of thought must be centered around the call of God and the redemption of mankind. We have not been called to do a natural work at all, but rather a supernatural work. We have been given a ministry of reconciliation. God, through His sovereignty, is allowing us to actively participate in the redemption of mankind.

Matthew 22:2
> *"The kingdom of heaven is like a certain king who arranged a marriage for his son..."*

Through His immeasurable grace, God has asked mankind to come into the sacred covenant of *marriage* with Him and become the *Bride of Christ*. He sends His servants out into the field as the *best man* of the *Groom* to proclaim the good news of His proposal. When they accept His proposal, we are commissioned to walk them down the isle of Discipleship, teaching them to observe all the things that He has commanded us.

2 Corinthians 2:15
> *For we are to God the fragrance of Christ among those who are being saved and among those who are perishing. 16 To the one we are the aroma of death leading to death, and to the other the aroma of life leading to life. And who is sufficient for these things?*

As one called by God, we are literally the fragrance of Christ among those who are being saved and among those who are perishing. But how will those who know not the Christ be exposed to this fragrance if we who are sent will not *Go*? Yes, there are those who will despise the very voice that we proclaim the Gospel with, but we must make it our aim to leave every man without excuse on the Day of Judgment.

Matthew 9:12
When Jesus heard that, He said to them, "Those who are well have no need of a physician, but those who are sick.

We have often referred to the church as a hospital for those who are sick, but how effective is the hospital with no ambulance? We as missional-minded believers are the paramedics that *Go* out into the field and rescue those who are injured, sick, or in danger of dying. The paramedic will perform CPR or whatever life stabilizing act that is necessary to sustain life on the way to the hospital. We have been called to go into the mission field as spiritual paramedics and speak the Gospel, a life-giving message to those who are dead in trespass and sin (Ephesians 2:1).

The truth is that most of our churches have become hospices, a safe place to go and peacefully await death. No healing, no hope, no abundance of life, just a place where like-minded people gather with no expectation of ever *Going* out. The mission and the function of a hospital and a hospice are different. The hospital seeks to save life, while the hospice provides a comfortable place to await death.

How is it that we say that we will win the lost through the love of Christ and never make an intentional effort to *Go*? The love of Christ is the very thing that leads us to *Go* into the world and preach the Gospel, the kind of love that should not allow you to keep your mouth shut when it is the very message of the Gospel that they must HEAR. This type of love will not allow you to stay within your controlled comfort zone where there is no missional work to be done. This type of love will consume you and drive you to *Go*.

So then, it stands to reason that we should now ask ourselves this question, do we truly love Christ? If we love Him, we will want to serve Him, and if we love Him, we will love His people, especially the ones in the *Urban Mission Field*. Perhaps we do not Go, because we love ourselves, our comfortable lives, our possessions, our status in society, far more than we love Christ. It is obvious that we have not fully understood the message of the Gospels and the instructions that we have been given.

Our membership list means nothing if we will not *Go*. If we will not recognize what time it is, our people will continue to be destroyed for the lack of knowledge. Their blood will continue to be upon our hands. It is 11:30, time to win souls. *We must Repent.*

Chapter Twelve

Romans 10:14

How then shall they call on Him in whom they have not believed? And how shall they believe in Him of whom they have not heard? And how shall they hear without a preacher? [15] And how shall they preach unless they are sent? As it is written: "How beautiful are the feet of those who preach the gospel of peace, Who bring glad tidings of good things!"

Beautiful Are The Feet

Have you ever wondered why the scriptures declare the feet of those who preach the Gospel to be beautiful? Could it be because these are the ones who bring the *Good News*, who *Go* into the world and make disciples, who literally fulfill the call of the *Great Commission*? Their feet are beautiful because they are found to be in the mission field just as Jesus was, just as the disciples were in the Book of Acts, preaching the Gospel to the lost and bringing the hope of salvation everywhere they walked. Are your feet beautiful?

How shall they hear without a preacher? Everyone in the church building has heard the Gospel, but what about those in the field? What about the ones who will not come to our churches? What about the ones who have grown up in other religions? Isn't it our responsibility as the church to bring the Gospel to them?

Romans 10:15 poses the question of "how shall they preach unless they are sent?" This is obviously not talking about being sent into the church to preach, but sent into the field to declare the Gospel to the lost. The problem today is not that we have not been sent, but how come we haven't gone. We have been commissioned for this work.

John 20:21
So Jesus said to them again, "Peace to you! As the Father has sent Me, I also send you."

Why won't we *Go*? Why does everyone associate being *called by God* with standing behind a pulpit? Why do we equate being a *preacher* with being a Pastor? Yes, a Pastor will be able to preach, but preaching was never intended to be contained within the walls of the church building. Additionally, preaching was never intended to be done only by the Pastor. Every member of The Body of Christ should be able to proclaim the good news of Jesus Christ. Just as Jesus was sent, He has sent us to *Go* into the world equipped with the Gospel and preach to those who are perishing and make disciples.

If Jesus spent most of His time in the mission field why do we feel that we have been privileged to do the work of the ministry within the confines of a building? Are we greater then, than our teacher? Have we found a better way? We must evangelize. We have been entrusted with such a glorious message, with such a purpose as to share it. We must *Go* and preach the Gospel.

When we look at our results, we have to face the conclusion that what we have been doing is not working. Our communities are getting worse, the nation has become less Christian, there are more churches closing their doors than opening. Our communities are a direct reflection of the Gospel that is not being preached. How shall they hear without a preacher?

Matthew 5:14
"You are the light of the world. A city that is set on a hill cannot be hidden. ¹⁵ Nor do they light a lamp and put it under a basket, but on a lampstand, and it gives light to all who are in the house. ¹⁶ Let your light so shine before men, that they may see your good works and glorify your Father in heaven.

How is it that we can claim to be the light of the world, a city set on a hill, but yet be hidden? Most people in our *Urban Mission Fields* know nothing of the ministry of the church. They have seen our monuments that we meet in, they have seen our billboards with images of our pastors, but they have not seen us. They have not seen us on their blocks walking amongst them. When a lamp is lit and placed under a basket, not only is it not visible to others, but eventually the fire will burn out.

We have adopted a treadmill form of evangelism. The treadmill creates the illusion that you are walking while you are actually staying in one location. Our pulpits have become the treadmill that we walk on and preach the Gospel from. We love the control, comfort, and flexibility that our treadmill gives us. We can change the speed at will, the incline at will, and it has become the great substitute to *Going* into the world.

But beautiful are the feet of those who preach the Gospel. There should be trails within our *urban mission fields* from the feet of those who are laboring and toiling. Instead the tares that the enemy has sown have overtaken the field. We can't even see the way because it has been forsaken for so long. It is time that we walk once again and restore the paths. *We must Repent.*

Chapter Thirteen

Mark 6:39
Then He commanded them to make them all sit down in groups on the green grass.

Make Them Sit Down

Discipleship has become a lost art form. No longer do we see an abundance of men of God who resemble the ones we read about in the scriptures. We have given ourselves to the ideology of not wanting to intrude into the lives of others. However the life of an evangelist or a witness is to do this very thing. We have been called to abruptly intrude into the lives of those who know not the Lord Christ Jesus and **"make them sit down"**.

One of the most overlooked elements in the feeding of the five thousand is not what they ate or how much was left over, but what

Jesus told His disciples to do. **"Make them sit down"**. There was no way that they would be able to feed the people unless they first made them sit down. In this same way of thinking, there is no way that we can feed people with the word of God unless we first make them sit down.

21st century Western Christianity, there is too much tolerance given to the constant drifting of believers. There is no accountability between the ministry and the spiritual growth of the members. The culture of the Church is consumer driven and seeks to fit unobtrusively into the schedule of the churchgoer. Our methods have arguably led to the lowest rate of spiritual maturity in church history.

> **2 Timothy 4:3**
> *For the time will come when they will not endure sound doctrine; but after their own lusts shall they heap to themselves teachers, having itching ears;*

People want a message that does not challenge their lifestyle. These people are "faith shoppers". If the pastor in church one condemns fornication in all of its variations, and they have a live-in girlfriend that they are not willing to marry, then they go over to church number two where the pastor is more lenient and tells them that fornicating with their girlfriend is between them and God. Now, their conversion requires no change in behavior, no sacrifice, no turning away from sin, and the "faith shopper" has just found a new church home.

Recent studies have shown that less than twenty percent of Americans attend church on a regular basis. This is horrific once you take into account what percentage of this small group actually practice what the scriptures teach. We are witnessing an epidemic before our very eyes. We have fostered a way of Christianity that is not at all biblical. Out of this small group of twenty percent, how many do you suppose are actually skilled in the word?

We have not made the people sit down. We have allowed them to wander from pillar to post, and they have become spiritually malnourished from a lack of food. It is not the responsibility of a new convert to find and prepare food, but the responsibility of the ministry to feed them. If we made the people sit down and fed them sound doctrine, "faith shoppers" would have nowhere to turn in their quest to find doctrine that supports their lifestyle.

1 Corinthians 3:2
*I fed you with **milk** and not with solid food; for until now you were not able to receive it, and even now you are still not able;*

New converts enter the faith as babes in Christ. They are in need of milk in the same manner that a newborn child in the natural needs milk. A baby is not capable of preparing food, so therefore they are solely dependent on their parents or caretakers for nourishment. It would be considered child negligence for a parent or caretaker to allow a newborn baby or infant to go without food.

Why do we allow so many of our new converts to go without food? Why do we abandon those who have just come into the faith and expect them to survive on their own? You see, we fail even in upholding the rules of our own doctrine. We refuse to Go, but we expect people to come to our churches. For this reason many of our new converts die in their infancy or they learn to survive by scavenging off of anything that seems edible. They begin to feast on strange doctrines, doctrines of demons, destructive heresies and the like and become unhealthy, spiritually diseased, and unfruitful for the works of the ministry. Babes in Christ **cannot** discern for themselves what is good and not good to eat.

Hebrews 5:13,14
For everyone who partakes only of milk is unskilled in the word of righteousness, for he is a babe. [14] But solid food belongs to those who are of full age, that is, those who by reason of use have their senses exercised to discern both good and evil.

It is clear that a newborn babe partakes only of milk. We cannot expect for a babe in Christ to have the same spiritual maturity as a believer who is full of age. Without the proper nourishment and care, a babe will never develop into a mature believer. The importance of this development is so that the believer will acquire the necessary senses needed to discern between good and evil.

If a newborn infant were to attempt to eat solid meat he would choke. No parent in his or her right mind would allow this. The natural progression would be to slowly introduce the baby to new types of food over time, allowing for the child to mature while giving time for his digestive system to adapt and develop. We would not expect the child to figure this out on his or her own. We would make the child sit down and eat. We would feed the child. We would nurture the child. Why do we expect such unrealistic things of newborn believers?

There are too many people exiting the backdoors of our churches. People come to church hurting, attempting to fill the void in their lives with something. The only thing that will fill the void is the word of God. Our cookie cutter three-point sermons are not going to get the job done. Just look around. Most of our churches have just as many people leaving as they do entering. People are looking for something, and even though they might not know what it is, we should. Until we make them sit down they will continue to walk out of the backdoor of our churches, still a babe and undeveloped.

> **Galatians 4:19**
> *My little children, for whom I labor in birth again until Christ is formed in you…*

Most women will tell you that the birthing of a child is the most painful but yet most joyous experience in life. The same can be said of making disciples. It is a work comparable to the birthing of a child. The labor that goes into it cannot be accomplished in the flesh. This is not a labor of studying or a labor of writing great sermons that Paul was referring to, but a one on one, hands on toiling and pushing and pushing until Christ is formed in a believer. This is discipleship.

It is the responsibility of the ministry to nurture and develop new converts and babes in the faith into productive, fruit-bearing, Christ-following disciples. This does not happen by chance. This is an intentional act of obedience to the word of God. There is no need to do evangelism if we are not going to do discipleship. There is no need to enter the Urban Mission Field if we are not willing to endure the labor of birthing disciples. We must make them sit down. *We must Repent.*

Chapter Fourteen

Mark 8:35
For whoever desires to save his life will lose it, but whoever loses his life for My sake and the gospel's will save it.

At All Cost

To be a Christian is to be a follower of Christ. When we look into the depths of the scriptures we realize that those who followed Christ were so convinced of the path that they were set on that they were willing to give their lives for Him and for His message. One will never experience what it is to be used by God in the manner that we read about in the scriptures until there has been this level of death to self.

One of the main things missing in ministry today is men and women of God who have died to self and given up all of who they are to become like Him, to become like Christ. There is too much flesh in the ministry. The Church was created to be a *no flesh zone* but has become a place governed by carnal, rational, and self-seeking motives. We seek not to lose our life but to save it. We look nothing like the men of old.

> **Mark 19:27**
> *Then answered Peter and said unto him, Behold, we have forsaken all, and followed thee; what shall we have therefore?*

This walk will cost us everything. If we are truly to fulfill the ministry that has been given to us, we must give up everything. All of self must be denounced until there is no self left. Our identity is found in Christ. We are to have the same mind of Christ. When this takes place we will begin to have the same desires of Christ.

The scriptures leave us more than enough examples of men of God who gave up everything for this walk. We should feel conviction when we look at the fruit that these men bore through the Holy Spirit and then look upon our ministries. But the difference between them and us is that they were willing to give up everything, while we set barriers and caps on how much of ourselves we are willing to give up.

Look around, there are places in which believers would never step foot. Places where it is evident that the Gospel is absent. We might pray for people but that is not enough. What stops us from taking the gospel to every corner? Is it our fear, or do we doubt that God will perform His word? Or is it that we are not really as sold out as we claim that we are? We should all take on the mindset that Paul had when it came to preaching the Gospel.

> **Acts 21:10-13**
> *And as we stayed many days, a certain prophet named Agabus came down from Judea. [11] When he had come to us, he took Paul's belt, bound his own hands and feet, and said, "Thus says the Holy Spirit, 'So shall the Jews at Jerusalem bind the man who owns this belt, and deliver him into the hands of*

the Gentiles.'" ¹² Now when we heard these things, both we and those from that place pleaded with him not to go up to Jerusalem. ¹³ Then Paul answered, "What do you mean by weeping and breaking my heart? For I am ready not only to be bound, but also to die at Jerusalem for the name of the Lord Jesus."

Paul had such zeal to fulfill this call that he was willing to lose his very life for the sake of souls coming to Christ. We are not even willing to lose our reputation, let alone our lives. The people must have thought Paul was crazy. Do people think you are crazy when it comes to fulfilling the call of ministry? Are you more like Paul or are you more like who society says you should be?

Many of us want to be conveniently used by God as if He were looking for part-time laborers. God has called us to be Co-Laborers in the field, serving alongside in the field with Him. We are not at liberty to set our own schedule or agenda. This is not a work at home gig. This is a fulltime, on call, 24 hours a day position. It calls for great sacrifice, but the benefits are vast.

1 Thessalonians 2:8
So, affectionately longing for you, we were well pleased to impart to you not only the gospel of God, but also our own lives, because you had become dear to us.

If we truly knew what was at stake, if we truly knew how glorious of a call this was, we would be throwing ourselves into the mission field begging to be used by God. Instead, we are led by the ritualistic cycle of what has come to be known as *church*. Look at our practices and look at the Word, they don't line up. Look at our results and look at the Word, they're not the same. Doesn't this bother you?

Philippians 2:17
Yes, and if I am being poured out as a drink offering on the sacrifice and service of your faith, I am glad and rejoice with you all.

Even though Missions and Marketing both start with the letter M, they have absolutely nothing in common. We can't just pop up and pass out flyers and expect a harvest, but we must post up and pour ourselves out as an offering amongst the people. A drink that has been poured out cannot be picked up, but it must be soaked up.

We must give of ourselves and spend the time necessary to build relationships that foster biblical discipleship. Have you ever stopped to think of how much time Jesus spent with His disciples? How much time do we spend with those whom God has entrusted in our care? 2 to 4 hours a week in most cases standing behind a podium.

> **Matthew 16:24**
> *Then Jesus said to His disciples, "If anyone desires to come after Me, let him deny himself, and take up his cross and follow Me.*

What has it cost you to follow Jesus? Have you become selfless? Have you totally denied yourself to the point where there is no more you? Many of those who profess to know Christ will never reach this level of self-denial nor desire to. Many will never give much of themselves besides the time it takes to go to a Sunday morning church service which makes them feel content and self-righteous in their walk with Christ.

We give ourselves to everything, careers, hobbies, relationships, and entertainment all in the name of self. Most of these things profit us nothing. Ironically, most of the things that we do in the name of ministry profit us nothing as well. There are few who have truly given themselves to this work.

The sad reality is that we aren't willing to lose rest, we won't set aside our plate for a time of fasting, we won't even come together for prayer to see where it is that God would like us to preach His Gospel. We have become blissfully content with our rituals. This is not church. This is not ministry. *We must Repent.*

Chapter Fifteen

> **1 Chronicles 4:10**
> *And Jabez called on the God of Israel saying, "Oh, that You would bless me indeed, and enlarge my territory, that Your hand would be with me, and that You would keep me from evil, that I may not cause pain!" So God granted him what he requested.*

Enlarge My Territory

The prayer of Jabez is one of the most missional appeals spoken in the scriptures. The Bible tells us that Jabez "called on the God of Israel saying, "Oh, that You would bless me indeed, and enlarge my territory". God only gives us territory for one reason, to carry out His will. We are blessed through our obedience and fulfilling the things that God has called us to.

God will not enlarge our territory for selfish ambitions. The only Kingdom that God is interested in building is His Kingdom. This is why you can have a church that sits on 40 acres of land with

25,000 people in weekly attendance, but yet they have no influence on the surrounding territory.

We have mastered the art of building models of the tower of Babel, which was an attempt to build upward to take on the appearance that they could reach heaven. However, we have utterly failed at building outward and influencing territory, which is a Kingdom concept that embodies the understanding that Heaven wants to reach us. God has called us to enlarge the territory of His Kingdom on Earth.

> **Matthew 10:7**
> *And as you go, preach, saying, 'The kingdom of heaven is at hand'.*

The Kingdom of Heaven is at hand and God's will is that His Kingdom would influence territory. When a country is invaded and conquered, the conquering nation changes the culture, language, and customs of the land and the conquered country becomes the territory of the conquering nation or Kingdom. The Kingdom of Heaven has come for such a cause, to conquer, influence territory and expand. If you look at our communities, no one would come to the conclusion that Christianity has conquered. Our communities remain, in large part, a culture of the flesh, where people hide their pain with addiction and the only language they understand is that of the almighty dollar.

> **Romans 15:20**
> *And so I have made it my aim to preach the gospel, not where Christ was named, lest I should build on another man's foundation…*

Paul made it his primary aim to preach the gospel in places where it had not yet been preached. Has this been our aim? Do we drive through the *Urban Mission Field* and pray that God will send all the dope dealers to jail or do we park our cars, take off our suits, and walk amongst them and preach the Gospel and set them free?

What we must understand is that what God has put inside of us, is the most influential and powerful force to ever come upon the face of the earth. The Word of God. God enlarges His territory through us, through evangelism, through the preached Gospel, but we must first *Go*. How can we expect to enlarge our territory from the inside of a building? Wars are fought on the field; strategies are made in the house. We must hit the field.

There is no reason that every church should not carry major influence in the territory that it exists within. Persecution is not even an excuse to default on this authority that we have been given to subdue and influence. When persecution arose in the Book of Acts the Word of God spread even more and the church grew greater in influence because these men at all cost were sold out for the Gospel. If persecution were to break out today, many of our churches would close their doors and the communities would not even miss their presence.

2 Corinthians 5:20
Now then, we are ambassadors for Christ, as though God were pleading through us: we implore you on Christ's behalf, be reconciled to God.

We have been sent as Ambassadors of the Kingdom of God. We do not come in our own name or our own power. An ambassador is a high-ranking diplomat that represents a foreign Government or Kingdom. So when we ask God to enlarge our territory, we are really asking Him to enlarge His territory through us. God will not enlarge our territory until we have first showed ourselves to be faithful over what He has already given us.

The end goal of missions is that the mission field would cease to be a mission field. We are to toil and labor in the field day and night, planting seeds and watering. When we have been faithful, in due season God will give the increase in the growth of the produce of the field. We then harvest what we have toiled and labored over in the field, lay a foundation, and take what has been gathered from the harvest and build it into a living tabernacle, therefore enlarging the territory of the Kingdom of God. This is missions, this is transformation, this is Kingdom. *We must Repent.*

Urban Mission Field

Chapter Sixteen

Urban Mission Field

Luke 9:62
And Jesus said unto him, "No man, having put his hand to the plough, and looking back, is fit for the kingdom of God".

Warning

The mission field is not for those who are not willing to forsake everything for the call. It's evident that there is a difference between those who believe and those who follow. Those who believe are satisfied with the fact that they have made the grand decision to believe that God exists and that Jesus Christ died for the sins of the world. On the other hand, those who follow desire to lose their lives, change their identity, and follow the Christ wherever He leads. Total self-denial. This is what Paul meant when he said that it is not I who lives but Christ who lives in me (Galatians 2:20).

If you are concerned with your own life, the mission field is not for you. If you are concerned with your own life, following Jesus may not be for you. If you are not willing to deny yourself, how can you follow Jesus? The Gospel makes it clear that there is an associated cost attached to following Jesus.

> **Luke 14:28-33**
> *For which of you, intending to build a tower, sitteth not down first, and counteth the cost, whether he have sufficient to finish it? ²⁹ Lest haply, after he hath laid the foundation, and is not able to finish it, all that behold it begin to mock him, ³⁰ Saying, This man began to build, and was not able to finish. ³¹ Or what king, going to make war against another king, sitteth not down first, and consulteth whether he be able with ten thousand to meet him that cometh against him with twenty thousand? ³² Or else, while the other is yet a great way off, he sendeth an ambassage, and desireth conditions of peace. ³³ So likewise, whosoever he be of you that forsaketh not all that he hath, he cannot be my disciple.*

Jesus was very upfront with people when they asked to follow Him. The last thing that is needed on the mission field is someone looking back. Jesus said that no man who has put his hand to the plough and looking back is fit for the Kingdom of God. That is a warning for any individual who dares step foot out onto the mission field. Ministry is not a game, and it is not to be taken lightly.

From a practical standpoint, when you plough a field, the furrows are made in a straight line, which demands that you look straight ahead, at some fixed point in the distance, to keep you on a straight path. You can clearly see how looking back will cause one to stray from the path. In the mission field, looking back is unacceptable.

The work that God has called His Church to do is too vital for double-minded men. You must be 100% sold out to Him and to

His work. To put your hand to the plough says that you are committing and submitting to His work. However, when one looks back, not only does he display that he is he not fit for the work, but he also displays that he is not fit for the Kingdom of God according to Jesus.

Hebrews 4:12
For the word of God is living and powerful, and sharper than any two-edged sword, piercing even to the division of soul and spirit, and of joints and marrow, and is a discerner of the thoughts and intents of the heart.

We can place no excuse in front of following Jesus. All intentions and selfish ambitions must be checked before we answer the call. While many may enter the mission field for the wrong reasons, God is able to discern even the hidden intents of the heart. Our motives must be pure or we will utterly fail in the eyesight of God. We may look like champions before men, but we will not be approved before God.

Many do this work just to say they are doing a work. Some do it for self-gratification, while others do it to be esteemed among men. We must do this work solely for the Glory of God. Even though the Gospel might be being preached, which in many cases it is not, after we have preached the Gospel we must make disciples, and in so doing fulfill the mission. Missions is preaching the Gospel and making disciples, period.

There are some who attach the word "Missions" to their work just to attract resources. Their campaign for resources far overshadows their campaign for souls, and if the resources run out, the work stops. This should not be. If resources come in they launch greater campaigns to attract even more resources. They seek notoriety, fame, and self-glorification. From such men remove yourself.

2 Corinthians 2:17
For we are not, as so many, peddling the word of God; but as of sincerity, but as from God, we speak in the sight of God in Christ.

The sad reality is that many pervert the work of God for selfish gain. The warning is that such a crooked path is easy for one to stumble down if they do not protect their heart. The deceitfulness of riches is a powerful force that lures even the strongest men so subtly away from their rightful calling. Godliness is not a means of gain, but godliness with contentment is great gain (1 Timothy 6:5,6). We must stay on guard at all times.

Philippians 4:11-16
I know how to be abased, and I know how to abound. Everywhere and in all things I have learned both to be full and to be hungry, both to abound and to suffer need. [13] I can do all things through Christ who strengthens me. [14] Nevertheless you have done well that you shared in my distress. [15] Now you Philippians know also that in the beginning of the gospel, when I departed from Macedonia, no church shared with me concerning giving and receiving but you only. [16] For even in Thessalonica you sent aid once and again for my necessities.

A missionary cannot lose sight of the call. Resources or no resources the work must be done. This must be the mindset of the missionary. We must learn to be both full and hungry, both to abound and suffer need. There are souls that hang in the balance and a glorious Gospel to be preached. If we are doing HIS work, HE will sustain us.

John 4:31-34
In the meantime His disciples urged Him, saying, "Rabbi, eat." [32] But He said to them, "I have food to eat of which you do not know." [33] Therefore the disciples said to one another, "Has anyone brought Him anything to eat?" [34] Jesus said to them, "My food is to do the will of Him who sent Me, and to finish His work

The true missionary is not discouraged in the face of lack. A lack of resources means nothing for such men. The work will continue to go on, resources or not. The true missionary is not in it for the money, fame, or notoriety. His fulfillment comes only from doing the work of GOD. HIS Work is our food. HIS Spirit is our resource. HIS Glory is our motivation. *We must Repent.*

Chapter Seventeen

> **Joel 2:17**
> *Let the priests, who minister to the LORD, Weep between the porch and the altar; Let them say, "Spare Your people, O LORD, And do not give Your heritage to reproach, That the nations should rule over them. Why should they say among the peoples, 'Where is their God?'"*

Where Do We Begin

When looking at the *Urban Mission Field* it becomes evident that something must be done. We cannot depend on the government or any other social organization to bring transformation to our communities. This is the responsibility of the Church. We have been given the authority to do such works. So where do we begin?

The first thing we must do is REPENT. We must first realize the error of our ways and turn back to God. We must lead our churches into genuine repentance and change the way that we think about ministry. There must be sincere weeping between the porch and the altar for the people of God (Joel 2:17). There must be a desire birthed in our churches and ministry leaders to return to the ways of the master.

Radical must become the standard once again. We must get to the point where we realize that radical isn't radical at all, but that it is the fundamentally expected norm for those who have answered the call of the Great Commission. We must stop justifying our Church activities as a substitute for evangelism. We must destroy the bondage of ritualistic church.

We must develop strategy. When we read the Gospels we notice that Jesus went from region to region spreading the Gospel. There was calculated strategy to His ministry. We should not evangelize where we do not plan on planting a church or where there is not a suitable church plant to disciple the new converts. If we desire to see transformation and revival in the *Urban Mission Field* we must develop strategy.

Our plan of approach will dictate our results. However, in the process of developing strategy we must pay close attention to what the Holy Spirit is saying. Any plan created outside of the guidance of the Holy Spirit will not produce Holy Spirit fruit. We must seek His guidance in where to *Go* and when to *Go, and in so doing, we* will see a harvest like never before if we execute His plan for evangelism and missions.

Believe it or not, the hardest part about evangelism is the part that says, *"Go"*. Once we *Go* and fulfill our obligated obedience to the Great Commission, God will do the rest. We must simply be willing vessels. But this must be taught. We must teach and send, teach and send, teach and send, creating an expectation of residual evangelism amongst those who serve in our Churches.

The reason most of our churches do such a poor job at reaching the people in the *Urban Mission Field* is because they have not been operating as a church, but merely as charitable organizations. An organization can grow in members and resources but only the Church will grow in evangelism and missional work. An organization has a limited target audience, but the church has the potential to reach all people.

Too often we get caught up in looking at the issues in our communities and attempt to solve them in a practical manner. The real issue in our communities is SIN. Sin is the common denominator amongst most of the issues that plague our communities. The only answer to that is the Gospel of Jesus Christ. So when the question arises in our Churches of where do we evangelize, or where do we plant, the answer is and always will be, where is the sin? The light is more needed where the darkness dwells.

We don't need more social programs in our communities, we need more Gospel. We need more men and women of God willing to walk through the streets of our communities and be fishers of men, aiming straight for the "lostness" that exists within the *Urban Mission Field*. If we continue to set up practical programs just to meet the practical needs of people, we will continue to get the same practical results. Not that the programs are bad, but usually we just end up with lost communities with more programs.

There must be an organic movement within the church that seeks to eliminate all impurities, preservatives, and false stimulants. We must simplify church back to its natural state to where the ordinary man can thrive, grow and duplicate. Biblical evangelism and discipleship must once again become the ingredients of our ministries.

We must make our presence seen, felt, and heard within the *Urban Mission Field*. The people must know and expect us to be there amongst them. We must get to the point where we spend more time in the field than at the church building. If we spend more time at church service, meetings, and conferences than we do in the field, something is wrong. We must break the *church service time* padlocks off of the ministry and become the church that we read about in the Book of Acts. We must declare His Glory among the gentiles.

We must understand the demographics of the field. This consists of understanding the people group in which we are ministering to. As missionaries we do this so that we can communicate the Gospel through their culture and language. This is not to be confused with using demographics for marketing tactics. We don't market the Gospel we preach it.

The common denominator that unites all demographics is sin. We can never feel that we cannot reach a particular people group because of their race, gender, or culture. The bottom line is that we preach a Gospel that is able to reach even the most destitute of souls. When this fact is understood, every mission field becomes a viable target for ministry. But above all, we must be led by The Holy Spirit in our *Going*.

The absolute best starting point that can be found is on our knees in the posture of prayer. This type of work cannot be accomplished without the consistent prayer of the saints. It would be of extreme importance for those who serve in the ministry to come together on one accord in a season of fasting and prayer. If we are going to expect results there must be a sense of desperation on the behalf of the Church.

We must be willing to step outside of our comfort zone and engage in a form of ministry that may be traditionally uncomfortable for most. We must catch on fire for the things that God desires. We must strive to imitate the Church that we observe in the book of Acts. We must change the way that we think about ministry. *We must Repent.*

Urban Mission Field

Urban Mission Field

Other Resources By J.L. Shelton

Books
Urban Mission Field: Tactical Field Guide To Urban Missions
The Foundation: The Elementary Teachings of Christianity
Logos: A comprehensive study of the literal "WORD" of GOD
Recycleship: A simplified look at the art of Discipleship

DVD's
Urban Mission Field
The Black Tape Letters
Testimony
The Mis-Education of the CHURCH
Recycleship: A simplified look at the art of Discipleship

CD's
Change Gonna Come
Spiritual Exodus Vol. 1-3
Revival

www.PastorJ.com
www.Day50Publishing.com
www.UrbanMissionField.com

About The Author

"Make Disciples"... This simple statement that Jesus commanded His followers has been the driving force behind the ministry of Pastor J. L. Shelton. The structure of his work has been built around being a servant-leader, leading from a position of servitude and equipping men & women of God to - participate in the redemption of mankind. His passion has been to reach the unreached and those who are not usually targeted by the traditional methods of outreach.

Pastor J is a devout student of the Word who finds a fervent love in the teaching of the Scriptures. Although he does not boast or find affirmation in his education, Pastor J has obtained multiple degrees in his journey over the years. He currently holds an Assoc. Degree in Multi-Media from the Art Institute of Houston, a Dual B.S. Degree in Theology & Christian Ministry from The College of Biblical Studies, a Masters Degree in Education-Curriculum & Instruction and he has also been a student of Religious Studies and Psychology at the University of Houston.

Over the years God has molded Pastor J in such a way that modern day "Churchology" would label radical and extreme. Having a heart of a missionary, he has taken the message of the Gospel and aimed it at a culture that has grown dull and de-synthesized to the voice of the Church. Pastor J has stepped out of the box of tradition and sought to walk in the likeness of the Church found in the Book of Acts. He has chosen to take the Word of God literally in all areas and seeks to "Make Disciples" that "Make Disciples".

It has been through his wrestling with God experiences that a hunger and thirst for the presence of God in his life and ministry were birthed. The vision that God has given Pastor J is one of Revival. A vision of the full restoration of the Glory of God once again resting upon the Church. A vision of the Church fulfilling its evangelistic call of preaching the Gospel to every creature. A vision of the Church united in the unity and love of Jesus Christ & absent of all denominational boundaries.

To Schedule Pastor J for a speaking engagement you can contact him personally at J@PastorJ.com

Urban Mission Field

www.ingramcontent.com/pod-product-compliance
Lightning Source LLC
Chambersburg PA
CBHW071722040426
42446CB00011B/2177